PORTRAIT PHOTOGRAPHY

MASTERING THE ART

Disclaimer

Contents

ESSENTIALS OF A GREAT PORTRAIT

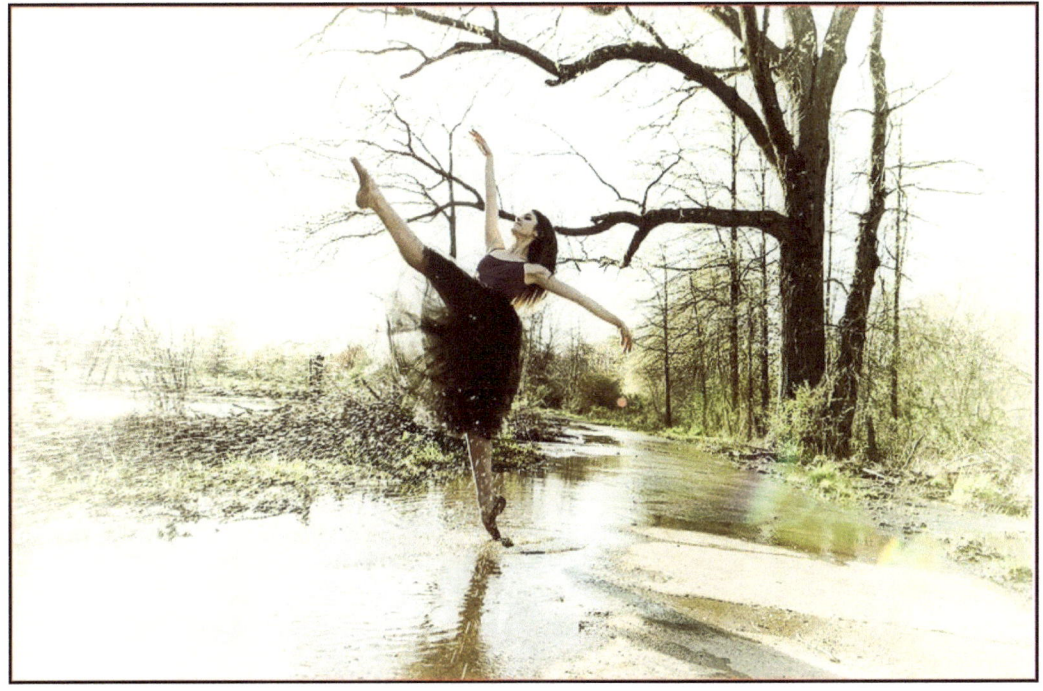

Figure 1 Capturing the essence of portrait photography

AESTHETIC QUALITIES OF A GOOD PORTRAIT

When you take a portrait, what do you want it to be? You want it to capture the personality of the subject, the essence of the surroundings and tell the entire story, all in one shot. Just as in the photograph above, the beauty, grace and passion of the ballerina is captured, with perfect lighting and a soft glowy effect, which gives the shot a fragile effect. This is what is called the perfect portrait photograph. A good portrait needs to have the following characteristics,

ARTISTIC SKILL

A great portrait needs to display the artistic prowess of a photographer. Communicate what you observe as an artist, and translate it into your portraits. Some expert photographers go for a relaxed natural look, while others tell their story through the display of elegance and softness.

Capturing the expression of the subject and directing the right pose are keys to getting a great portrait. Your portrait needs to be the best interpretation of your subject, and something more.

LIVEN UP THE SHOT

When you liven up the shot, it transcends time, and viewers are able to relate to it on an emotional level. It is your job as a photographer, to make sure to bring out the best in your subject for the portrait. Only then will your portrait be something more than a mere photograph by an amateur.

TELL THE STORY

The perfect portrait tells the story. Period. Capturing the portrait of the subject in such a way that the pose, expression and the surrounding all convey the essence of their personality is what portrait photography is all about.

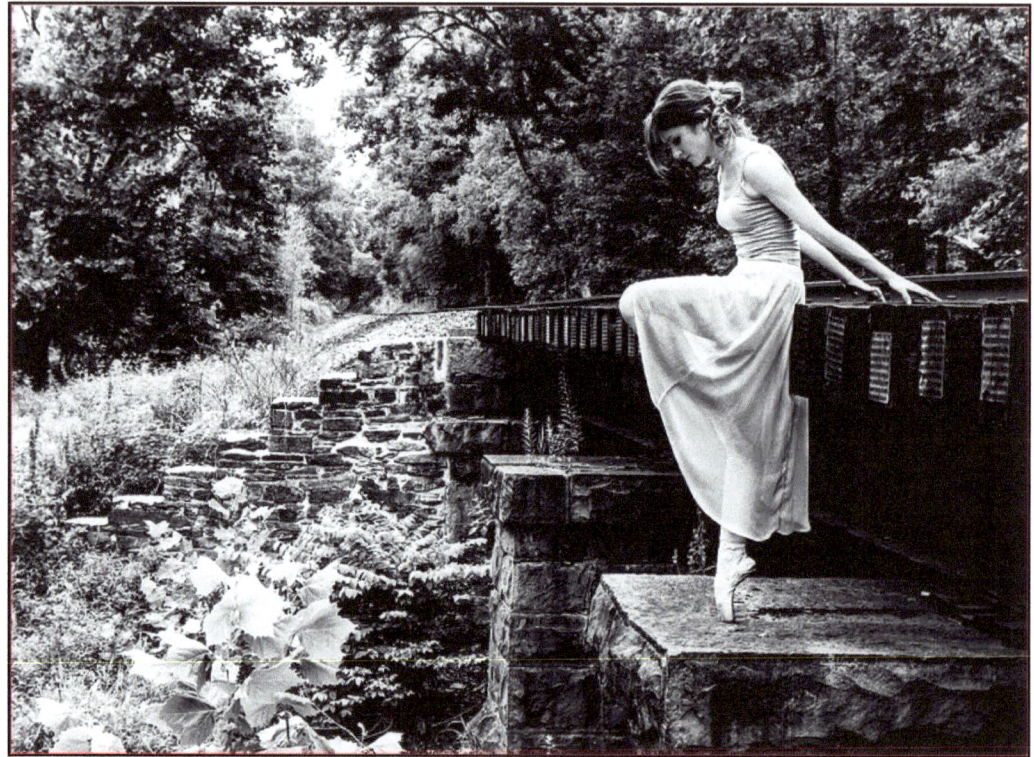

Figure 2 The passion for dance is a story in this portrait

MAKING MEMORIES WITH PORTRAITS

Perfect portraits make fond memories and live forever. The portraits include the history, environment and the personality of the subject, and capture and enclose it into a time capsule to be viewed and enjoyed time and again.

TECHNICAL QUALITIES OF A PORTRAIT PHOTOGRAPH

Aside from what a portrait needs in aesthetic value, the most important element of what a portrait requires is technical finesse, to make it into a work of art. Pay attention to the following technical qualities for a portrait.

PHOTOGRAPHY TECHNIQUE

To capture the perfect portrait, the photographer needs to show excellence in technical skills, related to posing, lighting and the overall effect with capturing the expression of the subject. This guide has instructions on how to get the perfect pose and lighting for your portraits.

CAPTURING THE EXPRESSION

What makes some portraits great works of art and masterpieces compared to others? The essence and magic lies in the skill of capturing the right expression, which tells the story of the subject's personality, feelings and mood. Eyes are considered to be one of the most alluring and compelling part of the human face, and many great portrait photographers focus on these to provide a window into the soul of their subject.

GIVE THE DETAILS THEIR DUE

What will make your portraits at par with expert photographers is how much attention you will give to details. How you blend tones, bring out or tone down the background, elevate the expression of the subject, use the pose to tell the story and the lighting effect to tell the complete story in your portrait, is what portrait photography is all about.

In portrait photography, the devil is indeed in the details.

If you want to know how an expert photographer captures the beauty and essence in portraits, ryancranephotography.com is the website to visit.

POSING FOR THE PERFECT PORTRAIT

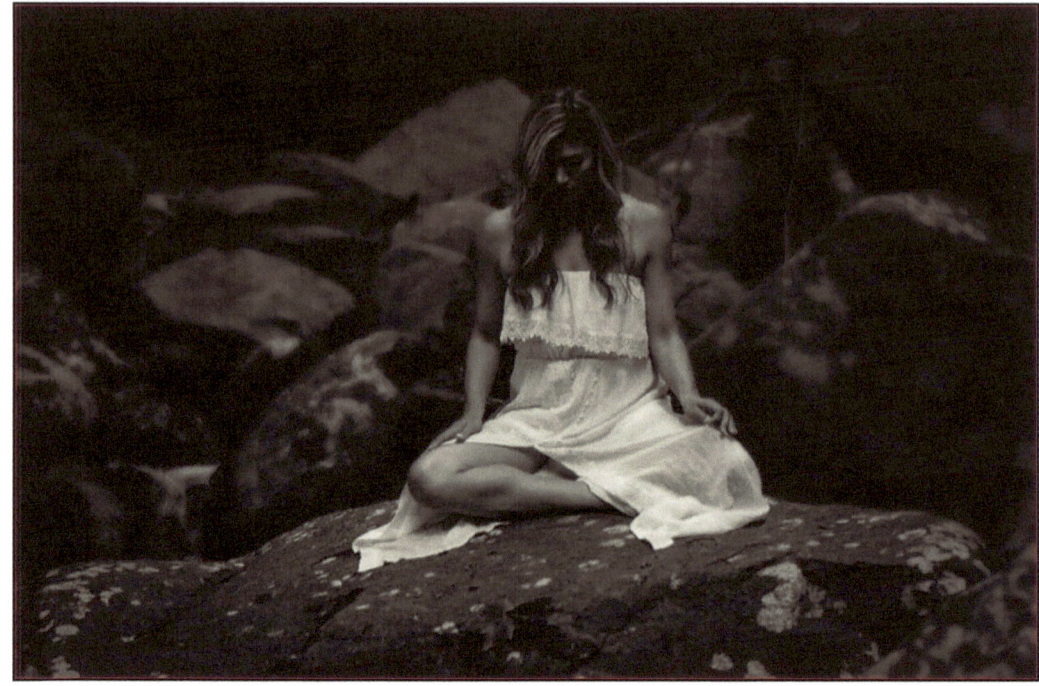

Figure 3 The right pose says it all!

When it comes to portrait photography, there are some who defy the traditional poses, while others stick to the classics. Whatever pose a photographer chooses for a portrait, depends upon their interpretation of the subject and the story they want to tell. There are two basic rules which need to be adhered to while choosing a pose for a portrait. These are:

- The pose needs to appear natural for the portrait
- The subject's features should not be distorted

Aside from these two basic rules, a portrait photographer is free to spin their magic and tell the story the way they want.

EVALUATION OF THE SUBJECT'S FACE
Before deciding on the right pose for the portrait, it is critical to evaluate the face of the subject in detail. The face of the subject should be studied under a flat light. Starting from a straight on study of the face, move towards the right side to study the subject from one angle. Then study

the subject's face from the left side. During the analysis of the face, a photographer studies the face to ascertain:

- What would be the best flattering angle to photograph the subject? The three quarters or seven eighths facial view gives better results compared to an in profile or head on pose.
- Some people don't have eyes of the same size. By angling the camera closer to the smaller eye, a natural effect is given which makes both the eyes look similar in size.
- Using an angle which reveals the high or pronounced cheekbones of the subject.
- Different angles can bring about a pleasant change in features, like a slim face may look wider from a head on angle etc.
- Determine the best angle and the ideal expression which adds value to that particular angle.

OPTIONS FOR PORTRAIT LENGTHS

The right pose is the key to an ideal portrait. You can tell a story and convey the feelings by positioning your subject in the right pose. There are many techniques and positions for portrait lengths, and subject views, which a portrait photographer can explore to pin down the effect they want for every photograph.

In the above image, the model has adopted a pose in which her body and face show a calm and peaceful expression. The portrait tells the story that the subject is at peace with nature, as the photographer has captured the essence of the background as well as the tranquil emotions of the model.

There are different lengths and poses to explore for getting an ideal portrait.

THE THREE QUARTER LENGTH

When a photographer decides to take a three quarter length photograph of a subject, the portrait reflects the image of the subject from the head and leading down to a point below the waist. The portrait usually consists of a photograph with the head of the subject leading most commonly to the mid thigh or mid calf region.

One very important element of this portrait length is the area in which the body of the subject passes out of the image edge. It is one very critical concern in this particular type of portrait. The reason being, that the portrait edge which shows the subject passing out of the frame may have an incongruous psychological impact on the viewer.

This is why, in order to avoid creating any unnerving or alarming psychological impact, it is highly recommended not to compose a three quarter portrait in which the edge of the frame actually falls at a joint of the subject.

GOING FOR THE FULL LENGTH SHOT

If a photographer aims for a full length portrait, the result is a print which shows the subject from head to toe. In this type of portrait length, there is usually a fair amount of background or the environment is also included besides the subject itself.

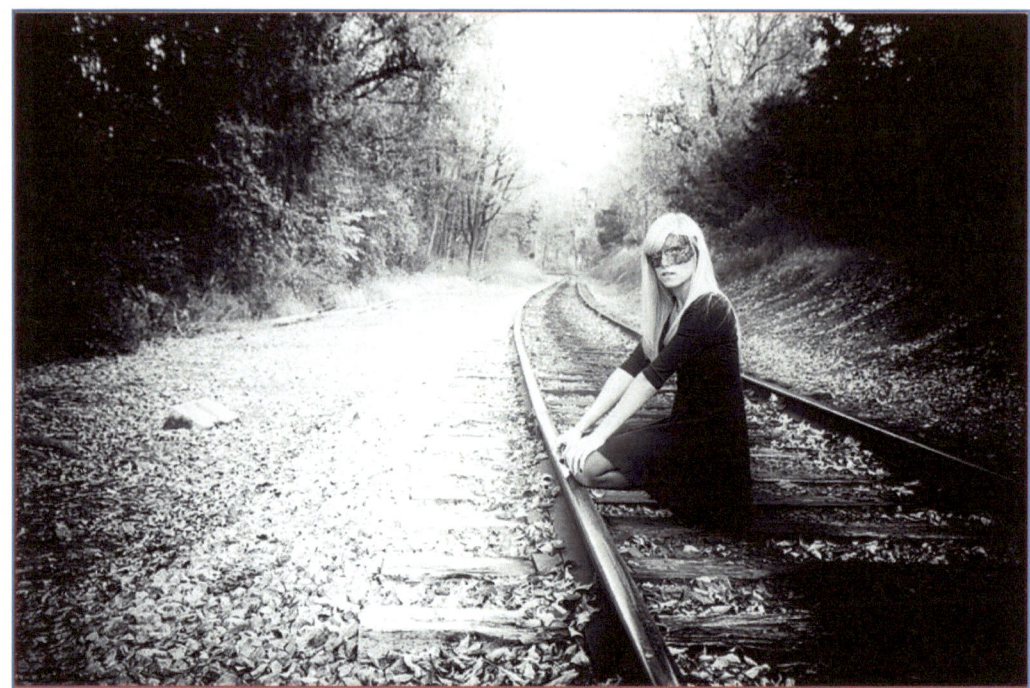

Full Length Portrait with a Complimentary Background

In order to capture the best portrait of a subject, while aiming for a full length shot, make sure that the background is chosen to actually enhance the appearance of your subject. The chosen background should not distract the viewer from the main focus of the portrait. Rather, it should add on to and compliment the subject as much as possible.

CAPTURING THE HEAD AND SHOULDER VIEW

One of the simplest types of portrait length is the portrait capturing the subject with the head and shoulders. This type of image shows the subject from the head down to the area just below the shoulders. The image may also include the subject being captured from head right down to the waist sometimes.

In this particular type of portrait length, the shoulders of the subject are focused on, to form the base, which leads the viewer of the portrait to the face of the subject.

Whichever type of portrait length is chosen, it is important that the photographer keeps the essential tips in mind so that the captured images appear pleasing, and pack a pleasant and forceful psychological impact.

FACIAL VIEWS FOR AN IDEAL POSE

Once you have decided on the ideal portrait length for your subject, the next step would be to choose a suitable facial view for it. There are three main facial views for capturing a meaningful and focused portrait, and are used for all types of portrait lengths. It is very important to note that irrespective of the type of facial view you choose for your portrait, the shoulders of the subject should also be posed at a specific angle to the camera. The ideal angles for the shoulders will be discussed later in this book.

THREE QUARTER FACIAL VIEW

This is one of the most versatile and most preferred facial views of all, for portrait photography. To create a portrait with a three quarter facial view, the subject is turned in such a way that the far ear seems hidden from the camera. More of one specific side of the face is visible in the portrait.

It is important to note that while the subject is turned away a little for the shot, they should not be turned so far to the side that the tip of the nose is seen to extend well beyond the cheek line.

Another tip is to make sure that the eye of the subject, which is on the side of the face turned farther away from the camera, is contained in the face with a small piece of skin that is visible all along the far temple. If a photographer notices that no such skin is visible in the pose, then it is recommended to turn the face of the subject a little more towards the camera.

The distance from the camera, makes the far eye seem smaller than the near eye, in a three quarter facial view portrait. Since people often have one eye that is smaller than the other, this effect can be minimized and a balanced portrait can be captured by positioning the subject in such a way that the smaller eye is nearer to the camera. This way, both eyes of the subject will appear to be of the same size in perspective, within the portrait.

POWER OF THE SEVEN EIGHTHS FACIAL VIEW

This facial view is captured with the subject looking slightly away from the camera. In this facial pose, the subject can be viewed with one side of the face more visible than the other one, through the lens of the camera. One point to note is that with a seven eighths facial view, the photographer will still be able to see both ears of the subject.

A PROFILE VIEW

In a profile facial view, the head of the subject is turned at about 90 degrees towards the camera. Only one eye of the subject is visible in the portrait. When arranging a pose for a profile facial view, have the subject turn their head away from the position of the camera. The head needs to be turned away until the far eye as well as the eyelashes completely disappear from view.

One tip for capturing a good portrait with a profile facial view is that if the far eye, especially the eyelashes are not visible to you, then you have arranged a great profile pose for a fine portrait.

POSING OF THE HEAD AND FACE

The right pose of the subject can actually make or break a portrait. With the right pose, the essence and feelings of the subject may be captured breathtakingly. There are many poses, and portrait photographers use them all to tell a story, capture a feeling or present a subject in a way they want.

TILTING OF THE HEAD

The subject's head should be slightly titled in the portraits, so that the natural line of the eyes is slightly slanted. If the face is not tilted, then the implied eye lines appear straight and parallel to the photograph's bottom edge. This results in a static composition.

For a dynamic pose, tilt the person's face so that the implied lines appear diagonal, for an ideal portrait.

THE MOUTH

While capturing a variety of portraits in different poses, some frames will reveal smiles while others will have serious expressions. A naturally smiling subject will produce a great pose for a portrait as the eyes will also be engaged in the smile for a perfect look. It is important that the subject is relaxed with no tension in the mouth muscles, as it gives an unnatural and posed look.

Photographers also need to take care of the laugh lines which appear usually on the front area of the cheek. In some cases, it might be required to increase the intensity of the fill light, so that the deep shadows can be lightened up. Another tip is to adjust the key light so that it is more to the front.

THE CHIN

The position of the chin is critical, as a chin which is too high will give the subject a haughty look. A chin held too low will present a look of low confidence and timidity. A high chin will make the neck look too elongated and stretched, while a chin held too low will give the impression of a double chin or as if there is no neck at all. For a natural look, opt for a medium chin height.

THE NEED TO ENGAGE THE EYES

The eyes are the most expressive part of the face. Thus, capturing a great portrait depends on how well you capture the feelings in the subject's eyes.

Make sure that the subject is relaxed and looking at the camera without hesitation. A relaxed subject will reveal an interesting pose and an ideal portrait.

ASSESS THE PUPIL SIZE

The pupil size is important, as bright lights will make the pupil appear really small, giving the subject a beady eyed look. Have the subject close their eyes just before the exposure so that the pupil size returns to normal for a good expression. Likewise, if working in a surrounding with dim light, the pupils of the subject will appear too large, giving a vacant eyed look. The trick is to ask the subject to look at a bright source of light for some time, thus restoring the pupil size to normal.

CHECK THE POSITION OF THE IRIS

It is important that the iris is captured bordering the eyelids. The space between the bottom and the top of the iris and the eyelid, should not have much white in between. If any white space is left between the iris and the eyelid, it should be done so intentionally in order to give a particular look and capture a pose. For example, if a photographer wants to capture a subject with a wide eyed innocent look, then suitable white space maybe left, otherwise not.

ARMS AND SHOULDERS POSE

The right pose of the arms and shoulders is important. Keep the following points in mind:

AXIS OF THE HEAD AND SHOULDERS

The shoulders of the subject should be positioned at an angle to the camera for all facial views. Shoulders facing the camera make a person look wider than they are. While photographing men, the head and shoulders are generally turned in a similar direction, while for women the head is at a different and opposite angle to the shoulders.

TRIANGULAR BASE LINE

The arms should not drop down from the shoulders, but rather, should be projected a little outwards to give sloping gentle lines with a triangular base for an ideal composition. Another way to capture the triangular base is to having a posing table to rest the far elbow.

THE SLOPING LINE

The line of the shoulders must not be parallel to the ground, whether the subject is standing or sitting. One shoulder must be positioned a little higher than the other. This creates a pleasing sloping line effect.

CAPTURING HANDS IN GROUP PORTRAITS

In portraits, hands appear larger in size due to the fact that they are closer to the camera. A photographer can use a longer than normal lens to make the size relationship between the face and hands appear normal. Never photograph hands facing the camera, as it distorts the shape and size of the hands. One other tip to photograph the outer edge of a hand is to give a flowing natural line to the hand. Some important tips to keep in mind are:

- Photograph with a wrist slightly raised so that there is a gentle curve line and smooth bend where the hand joins the wrist.
- To give the fingers definition and form, photograph them with a slight separation in between.
- To give roundness and dimension to the hand, have the subject hold something small so it's not a fist.
- Either photograph the entire hand or show none of it. It is good to hide the hands in the pockets or to keep them in the lap. Too many hands pose distraction.

SUBJECT HANDS IN STANDING POSES

A standing subject can have the arms folded across the chest for a strong good pose. A man can turn his hands in a slight way, so that the hand edge is more visible. To give the arms a slimmer look, have the subject hold the arms out from the body.

A woman with a hand at her side and the other on her hip is a good pose. Keep the free hand twisted to give the hand a soft elegant look.

HOW TO AVOID ANY DISTORTION

To capture the perfect portrait, it is essential to avoid any distortion. Here are tips on how to do that,

ADJUSTING THE HEIGHT OF THE CAMERA

- For a head and shoulders portrait, place the camera at the height of the tip of the subject's nose.
- For a three quarter length, the camera should be placed at midway height of the waist and neck of the subject.
- For full length portraits, the camera is to be placed at a height of the subject's waist.

SETTING THE FOCAL LENGTH

- For a head and shoulders portrait, a short telephoto is a good choice, while for full or three quarter lengths, a normal lens can be used.
- If working room is available, then longer lenses will give good results. The use of extreme telephoto lenses should be avoided.

COMPOSITIONAL ELEMENTS OF A PERFECT PORTRAIT

These elements and tools weave an impact to compel the viewer through the image. Read on to know how.

UNDERSTANDING THE RULE OF THIRDS

The area of the dynamic visual interest is where any two lines of the rule of thirds diagram intersect. It is the ideal spot to place the main point of interest.

In a head and shoulders portrait, the eyes should be at the intersection of two or a dividing line of the viewing area of the rule of thirds.

In a full length or three quarter one, the head should fall on a dividing line or intersection point.

THE PORTRAIT DIRECTION

- Leave more space in front of the subject rather than behind them for a direction and movement effect.
- When capturing a subject looking toward the camera to the right, there should be more space on the right side of the frame.
- Even if the subject is to be centered in the mid of the frame, leave more space to whichever side the subject is turned.

USING THE LINES

It is important to identify and distinguish between real and implied lines.

THE IMPLIED LINES

These are not obvious lines, like the bend of an arm or curve of a wrist. These implied lines must not contradict the composition of the portrait but must modify it. They must add touches in the direction, leading to the actual point of interest.

USING THE REAL LINES

A real line is one which is obvious, like a horizon. Real lines must not intersect the portrait in two halves, as this will split the portrait composition into two pictures. Provide visual weight to the image by locating the real lines on a point which is one third into the photograph.

DIAGONAL LINES USED IN PORTRAITS

Diagonal lines offer a gently sloping path, which is followed by the eye of the viewer. These are not like natural vertical and diagonal lines and are thus more interesting.

INTRODUCING TENSION AND BALANCE IN THE PORTRAIT

Tension is a state of any imbalance in the portrait. One can create visual tension by pairing a small subject with a big sky. Balance is using two dissimilar shapes to create harmony in a photograph.

Usually tension is resolved in the image through the introduction of balance. Tension may also be referred to as visual contrast, with more subjects on one side of the portrait than the other, all with different sizes and shapes. An ideal visual balance may be introduced by either color coordinating between the different subjects according to their size or some other factor.

The eyes would see a balanced result if same sized subjects are wearing same colored clothing, and the toys or subjects on the other side are dressed in dark colors.

CHOOSING THE RIGHT SHAPE AND SUBJECT TONES

Using shapes and lines to get the triangular base or some other form for an ideal portrait is important. Shapes introduce balance and tension within a portrait, and subjects may be linked by creating any common element between different multiple groups. Shapes and lines are used to create well composed images which have the element of visual interest introduced by the photographer.

Bright tones advance on a visual level, while dark tones retreat. Light pictured elements in the picture will be distracting, so any bright areas on the edge of the picture should be darkened to avoid distraction.

DIFFERENT COMPOSITIONAL FORMS YOU CAN USE

The S shaped composition is a favorite in which the center of interest actually falls in the dynamic quadrants of the picture. The rest of the composition actually forms an S shaped sloping line, which is used to lead the eye of the viewer to the main interest area.

The L or inverted L shaped compositions are used for reclining or seated subjects. The Z and C shaped compositions are also visually pleasing and seen in different types of portraits.

For more details visit, ryancranephotography.com, and go to improveyourphotographyonline.com, to learn helpful tips from the pro.

CAPTURING THE EXPRESSIONS AND RETOUCHING PORTRAITS – THE ESSENCE OF MAGIC IN YOUR PHOTOGRAPHY

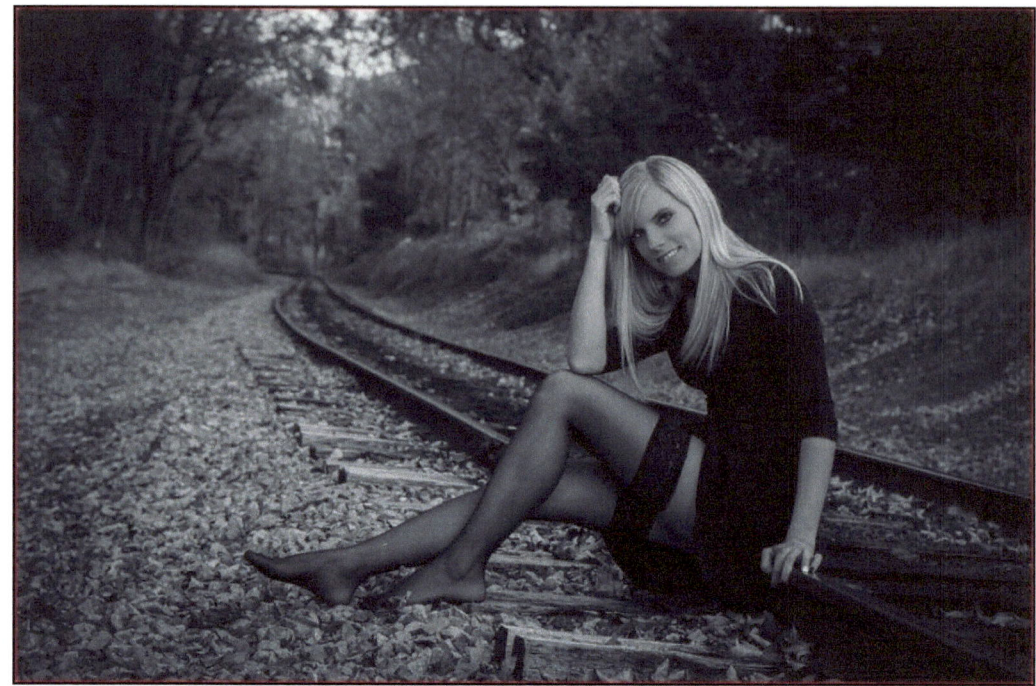

Capturing A Natural Expression

ELICIT THE RIGHT EXPRESSION

The right expression can make a portrait a masterpiece. If done professionally, the portrait itself becomes the expression. Experts suggest watching the subject and choosing any regular movement as their artistic pose. A natural smile is best and capturing the moment is ideal, compared to instructing the subject to force a smile or expression on their face. For the best results, it is important to study the subject carefully.

GO FOR THE SMILE FORMULA

Expert photographers suggest that natural smile is one where the subject smiles with their eyes. Anything less than that seems forced and artificial. The smile formula suggests making the subject smile so that they forget to focus on their actual smile and enjoy the moment, which would translate into an ideal expression in the portrait.

RETOUCH FOR THE BEST RESULTS

Retouching of photographs has been upgraded and digital retouching methods have not only made the process more time efficient but also promises more pleasing results, than the methods used before. Retouching is done to the digital file and the image is a positive, retouched and delivered to the customer.

Retouching in Adobe Photoshop lets a photographer to magnify any area of the image up to 1600 times. With a wide variety of erasers, brushes and pencils which can be adjusted to the opacity and transparency of choice, any detail in the images can be retouched. Facial irregularities and blemishes can be easily retouched and there is no limit to the complex effects that can be retouched digitally.

THE MAGIC OF LIGHTING IN PORTRAIT PHOTOGRAPHY

Magic of portrait lighting is to create a three dimensional illusion in a two dimensional medium, and illuminate the subject. Contouring of human faces and forms, illumination of skin textural qualities, an elevated sense of depth with balance in idealism and realism is all woven with lighting.

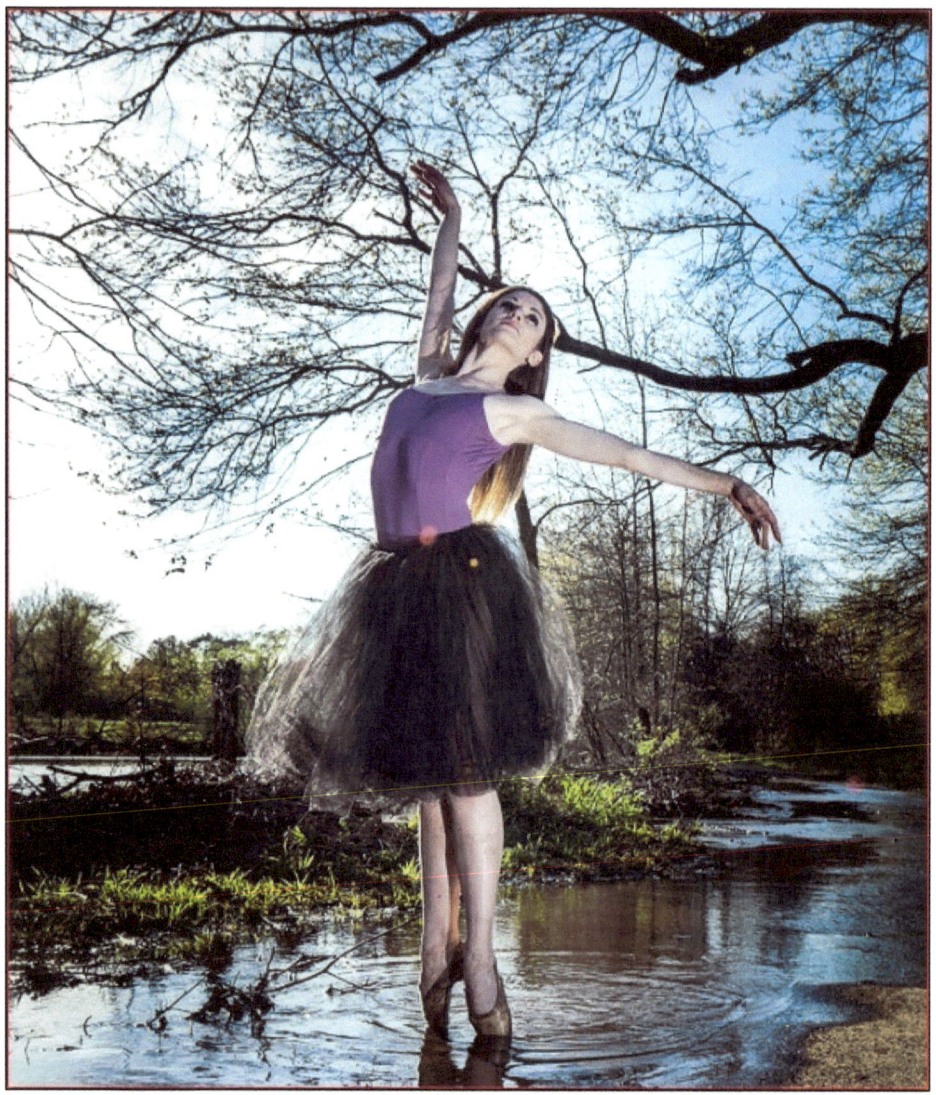

Illuminating the desired look with the magic of right portrait lighting!

KNOW YOUR LIGHTS WELL

Incandescent and basic flash electronic units are used for portrait lighting. A photographer needs to know their lights well to get desired results.

BACKGROUND LIGHT

A low powered light, it just illuminates the background to separate the background and the subject tonally. These are mostly placed on a stand behind the subject. It is out of the view of the camera lens. The lights may be placed on a high stand to be placed on any side of the set, directed towards the background.

FILL AND KEY LIGHTS

These lights need to be high intensity bulbs, that are set in parabolic reflectors. 250 to 500 watts is suitable for a small room, while 200 to 400 watts is a suitable power rating for portrait photography, while using electronic flash. Reflectors are silver coated inside to ensure maximum reflection of lighting, and light assemblies need sturdy support while diffusion is used like soft boxes or umbrellas.

If using undiffused key lights, these should be fixed with barn doors to control the beam width, light up only desired parts of portrait, prevent any lens flares and keep stray light off the lens of the camera.

The fill light should have a diffuser, attached with suitable room between it and the reflector, so that heat has a chance to escape. These should also have barn doors, and it is important to ensure that no light is spilled into any unwanted areas of the portrait scene.

KICKER AND HAIR LIGHTS

Hair and kicker are optional lights. Hair lights are small ones with a sealed down reflector and controlling barn doors. A reduced power setting is used since it is undiffused. These are used to illuminate hair, without any lens flare.

Kicker lights add highlights to the body or face sides, invoking portrait richness and enhanced depth. These are placed behind the subjects, and snoots and barn doors should be used.

DIFFERENT LIGHTING TYPES TO KNOW

SHORT LIGHTING

In this type, the light illuminates the face side that is turned away from the camera. It highlights facial contours, and also used as a technique for corrective lighting to narrow a wide or round face. Short lighting with a weak fill light can help produce a dramatic effect with deep shadows and bold highlights.

BROAD LIGHTING

This light illuminates the face side turned towards the camera. It is used less frequently, since it deemphasizes and flattens the facial contours. It is used to widen up a long or thin face.

KNOW YOUR BASIC LIGHTING SETUPS

PUTTING THE LOOP IN LOOP LIGHTING TECHNIQUE

In this type, the key light is lowered and placed to the side of the subject, as the shadows right under the loops form a small loop, to the shadowed side of the subject face. It is common portrait lighting and ideal for subjects with oval average faces.

The fill light is placed opposite the key light, on the subject/camera axis. The light should not cast any shadows and maintain the one character light feature. Check through the camera to see if fill light is casting any shadow. Hair and background lights are used similar to paramount lighting setup.

UNDERSTANDING PARAMOUNT LIGHTING

Called as glamour or butterfly lighting, it is popular as a feminine lighting pattern, which produces a butterfly like symmetrical shadow beneath the nose of the subject. It highlights good skin and high cheekbones. Not used on men as a general rule, since it has the effect of hollowing out eye sockets and cheekbones too much.

The light is placed quite high and infront of the subject. It is parallel to the vertical line of the nose. This lighting should not be used for subject portraits with deep eye sockets, as no light will be illuminating the eyes. The fill and key lights are on same side of face and a reflector is used on the opposite side to fill in shadows on the cheek and neck.

The hair light is placed opposite the key light, and only illuminates hair, not skims the face. Background light is behind the subject placed low, forming a semi-circle illuminated background.

SPLIT LIGHTING

Key light only illuminate half of the face of subject. An ideal slimming light, it is used to narrow a wide nose or face. A weak fill light is used to hide any facial irregularities. No use of fill light gives a very dramatic effect. The key light is placed lower and farther to the subject's side. In some cases key light maybe behind subject depending on their angle turned away from camera. Hair, background and fill lights are used in normal way.

REMBRANDT LIGHTING

Also called as 45 degree lighting, this setup involves a triangular small highlight falling on the shadowed cheek of subject. This is a dramatic and commonly regarded as masculine style lighting. A weak fill light is used to accentuate the highlights of the shadow sides. The key light is placed farther and lower to the subject's side. It comes from the side of the subject depending how far the face is turned farther from the camera. Fill light is used as in loop lighting, while the hair light is placed closer to subject to introduce brilliant hair highlights. Background lights are in standard position, and kickers are used in Rembrandt lighting. These add highlights to shoulders and temples and delineate the face sides. Avoid image degrading flare by making sure no lights fall on the camera lens. A diffused keylight blurs the triangular lighting and placement affects the high or low angle of the triangle light on the cheek.

FASHION LIGHTING

It is frontal and soft with a subject/lens axis. It does not model subject face, and makeup is used for that. It is stark lighting with a large softbox and a silver reflector held directly over and beneath the camera respectively. For a soft effect both reflector and light are placed close to subject. Catchlights in a fashion portrait are seen as a large one over the pupil, and one less intense under it. In some cases a circular catchlight is produced through a ring-light flash. The current style in fashion portraiture is bold, masculine and dramatic. Flat lighting is rarely used with men now, and side lighting with hard shadows are preferred.

PROFILE LIGHTING

Known as rim lighting, it is used when subject's face is angled 90 degrees from the lens of the camera. It is a dramatic lighting for highlighting elegant faces. Key light is placed behind subject to illuminate the profile, with a heavy light falling along the face edge and highlighting the subject's neck and hair.

The light accent should be centered on the face, not the neck and hair. Fill light is placed on the side similar to the key light, with a reflector to fill in shadows. Background light is normal and hair light is optional, placed on the key light side.

KNOWING YOUR LIGHT MODIFIERS

With the use of modifiers with the different lights, there are limitless variations, arrays and effects which can be produced in a portrait.

PARABOLIC REFLECTORS

It is a polished silver metal reflector, which has a strobe head or lamp attached. They produce well defined shadows, sharp light and a lot of contrast. Parabolics let one see and control light much efficiently than a diffused light source. The fill light should be fitted with a diffuser.

UMBRELLAS

These are white or silver and placed close to subject to create a directional soft light. A silver light umbrella is used as a key light due to its directness and intensity. A matte umbrella is used as a secondary or fill light.

SPOTLIGHTS

It is a hard edged light source which gives a defined shadowy edge, thus giving more shape to subject features than diffused and low contrast light sources. The light has a Fresnel lens attached, which focuses the spotlight, emitting a light beam which stays condensed even over a long distance. Barn doors are foxed to control spread of light, thus a selective area or corner with background can be lighted. Honeycomb grids are also used as key lights in this setup.

BARN DOORS

These are metallic black adjustable flaps that can be adjusted to control the beam width of a key light. These are used to light up selected areas, and keep stray light off camera lens.

ALL ABOUT LIGHTING RATIOS

It is the difference measured in intensity between the highlighted face side and the shadow. It is expressed in a ratio, with ratio of highlighted side of the face over shadow side. The ratio tells the local contrast of the portrait. 3:1 is a lighting ratio which is desirable for both outdoor and indoor portrait photography.

DIFFERENT TYPES OF PORTRAITS AND TIPS FOR IDEAL RESULTS

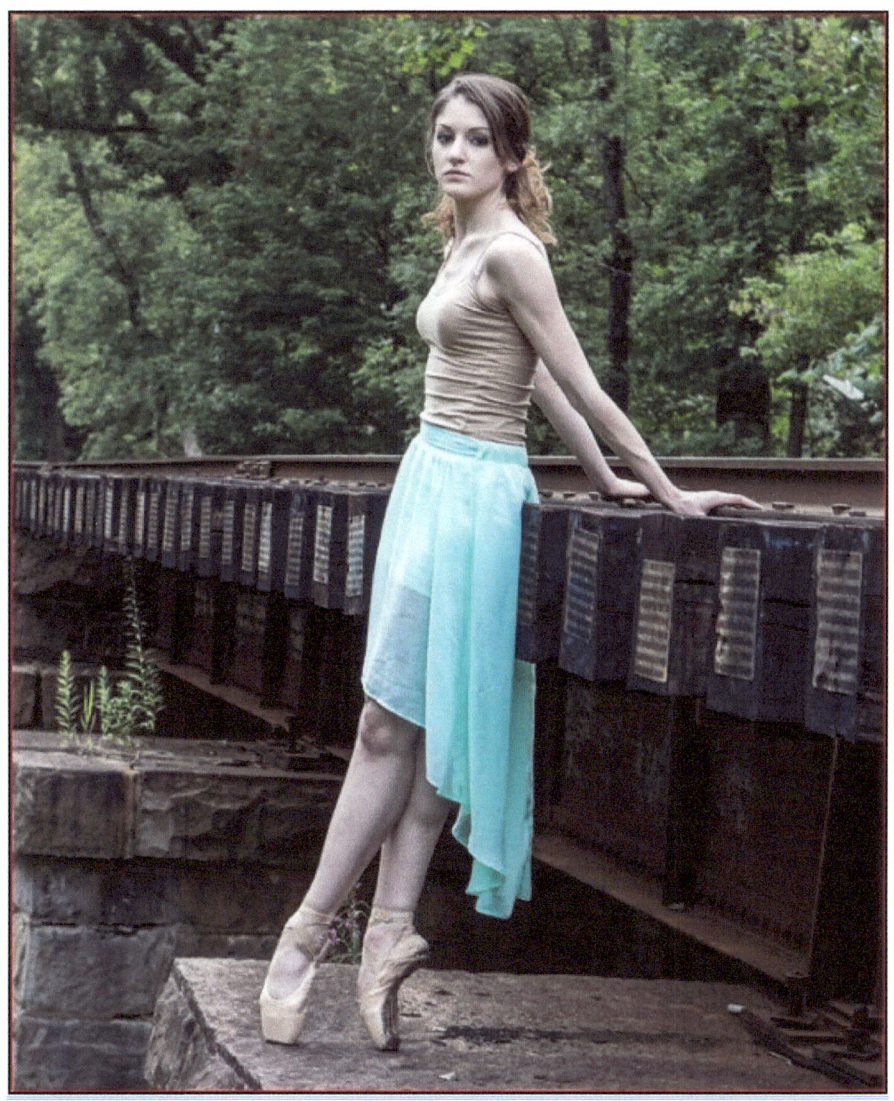

Capturing Perfect Portraits

FAMILY PORTRAITS

Family portraits may involve a young family and parents, or a shot of multiple families all within one.

ENSURE THE RIGHT POSE, LIGHTING AND CLOTHING

Coordination of clothing is essential for family members for a portrait. Neutral or cool colors are a good idea for clothing, since faces appear warmer and pleasing within the portraits. The family garments should blend, with shoe styles and colors blending in with the person's attire.

Posing can be done by age, size or with small family subgroups. The lighting needs to be even all over the group, so family groups can be captured with a soft light and an umbrella flash. Multiple umbrellas can be used and light reading all across the group from front to back and left to right should be identical. Shadows should fall behind the subjects, and not on other people. For outdoor portraits multiple lights might be needed.

CHILDREN PORTRAITS

Capturing perfect children portraits is a major challenge since it is not easy to control or instruct the young subjects. In children photography, it is ideal to use an assistant as well as props, like stuff toys, and rocking chairs, to attract the subject's attention and keep them happed and posed for an ideal photograph.

RIGHT LIGHTING WITH TRIPOD AND CABLE RELEASE ARE KEY

The basic lighting setups need to be used, and should be simplified for the active subjects, who have short attention spans. The placement and setting of elaborate lighting setups must be replaced with a single broad backlight, which produces an even effect all over a larger area. It is suggested to use only one light if possible.

Many photographers use cameras fitted on a tripod, with a radio remote or a long cable release, so that they are free to roam away from the camera. This way, they are able to interact easily with their subjects, and keep them relaxed to capture an ideal portrait. A loose composition is ideal to compensate the movement of the subject.

Clothing should be appropriate to the setting and coordination of the props, blankets and clothing is essential. Casual clothes in outdoor settings are a suitable choice. Clothing can be used to define the personality or outline the importance of a moment. Ensure child comfort though and don't be too specific on what is being worn.

GROUP PORTRAITS

Group photography is a daunting and challenging task for any photographer.

RIGHT POSING WITH PLANNING IS THE KEY

Planning for a large group photograph requires the right setting. It is important for a photographer to know the group makeup, reason for the photograph, and different ideas for organizing the group. The ideal lenses to be used should also be decided by the photographer, and they should be in charge of the project. A group portrait should have a rhythm and style. It is up to the photographer as to what way they want to organize and photograph a group for a portrait.

RIGHT VISUAL MOVEMENT AND PLANES

To create visual movement, it is important that no two faces in a group are on a similar plane. In a group portrait, every subject can have a pose on a different plane, as planning in terms of multiple levels, ensures that the group portrait appears pleasing to the eyes.

The closeness of the subjects in a group portrait is another important element. Closely arranged subjects imply closeness, which is linked to warmth. Distance between portrait subjects, gives a chance to introduce shapes and flowing lines, within the portrait composition. Whether loosely or closely arranged, consistency is the key, with equal distance between all members of the group.

One or many planes can be made for placing the group subjects. With these planes, the lighting is simplified, making it possible to include everyone in the depth of field of the lens. Some settings also give a natural organization for the planes. Subjects in the back and front should be close, so that all of them are captured with sharp focus. Each individual subject should do well as an individual portrait as well, as this is the judgment criteria for the quality of a group portrait.

POSING FOR COUPLES, LARGE GROUPS, GROUPS OF ODDS AND EVEN NUMBERS

In a couple setting, one subject is generally expected to be taller than the other. The mouth height of one subject must be at the lower subject's forehead height. Mouth to eyes height arrangement is recommended by many photographers. Couple can be posed in parallel positions or at a 45 degree angle with each other. Subjects facing each other makes for a good pose which creates a diagonal line, giving direction to the portrait.

In big groups, the photographer needs to focus attention on the basic elements of design, accentuate and highlight implied and real lines. Overlapping subgroups is a good way to add visual sense in a large group. Angling the subgroups towards one another is a way to bring uniformity in large group compositions.

It is tougher to photograph an even number of subjects compared to odd groups, as the brain naturally accepts the odd numbered disorder more readily than an even numbered one. Three member groups are pleasing as they give a diamond or pyramid shaped composition. In a small group, the face heights are adjusted to be at different levels, while the turn of the shoulder is a way of looping the group together. Groups of three or anymore subjects enable the photographer to add design, architectural and natural elements into the portrait.

ENVIRONMENTAL PORTRAITS

For these portraits the photographer needs to see and be able to control the lights.

OPEN LIGHTING AND SHADES

Portraits can be captured under a shade, but not outdoors. The ideal shade would be a porch, with open sides. This way, the shade will filter in light, not from overhead but from the sides, giving the light a gentle direction. Holding a gobo over the subject is a good way of blocking the overhead light.

AFTER SUNSET SHOTS

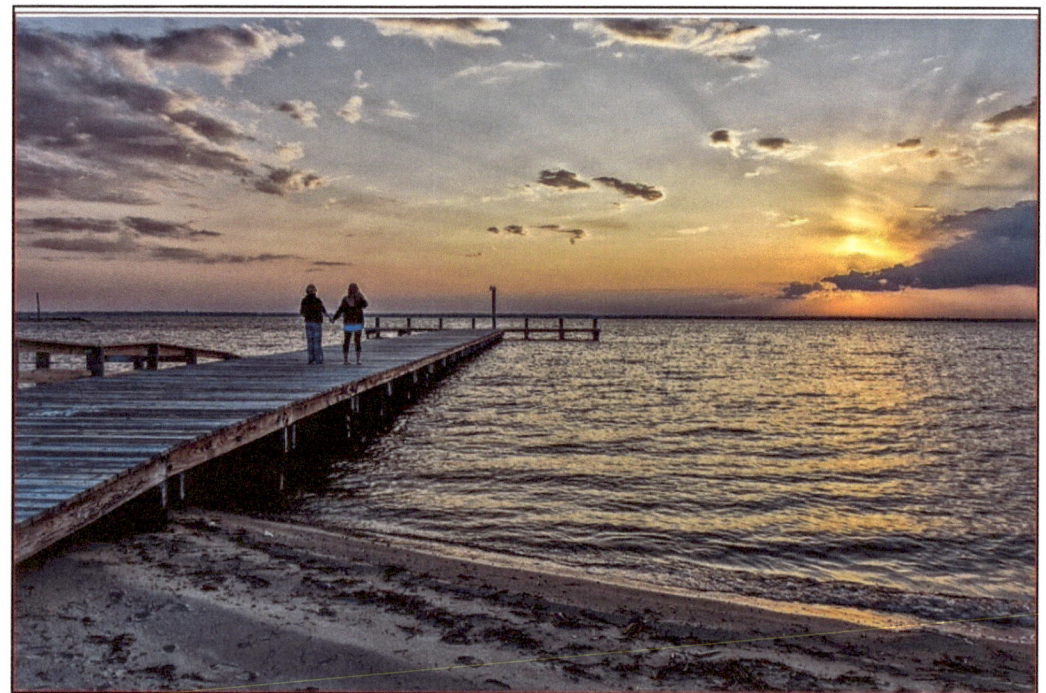

Capturing Beauty After Sunset

Great portraits can be captured after the sun has set, as the entire sky becomes a softbox, with soft and even lighting effects on the subjects, with no worry of harsh shadows. The three obstacles of working in this kind of light are that first, it is dim. High to medium ISO settings with slow shutter speeds will need to be used which can pose a challenge. The second problem is that subdued lights restrict the field depth, as you have to choose wide apertures. Twilight also does not produce any catchlights, because of which photographers use a flash, or a barebulb flash which produces twinkles in the eyes.

Since twilight changes so rapidly, it is difficult to work in it. Different lighting levels are produced and the photographer needs to use the meter repeatedly, in order to adjust the flash output.

EXECUTIVE PORTRAITS

With limited time available with the subject, it is good to be aware of the subject and their offices beforehand. Executive portraits are on location, and all the lighting paraphernalia needs to be taken to the offices for lighting up the executive and their surroundings. The setting should be typical and relative to the subject, and one which puts them right at the centre of attention. They should be at the focal point of the scene.

A wide angle lens and getting a close effect of the subject, is the right way to loop in the surroundings in the portrait. Limited space also makes wide angle a need.

WEDDING PORTRAITS

Different types of portraits are taken at a wedding and all should conform to the doctrine of sophisticated posing coupled with elegant lighting. The portrait of the couple should be of full length and three quarter length. Introduce dynamic lines in the composition, with the couple leaning in towards each other.

The portrait of the bride should be one full length and a head and shoulders length. The subject should be posed at an angle with the lens. The bride can have her head and shoulder tilted with the high shoulder giving her a feminine S curve.

FASHION PORTRAITS

These are different from conventional portraits, as the object is to bring out the beauty of the subject. With more frontal type of lighting, posing is more relaxed in nature, and close up images of composition are ideal for fashion portraits with a tight cropping feature.

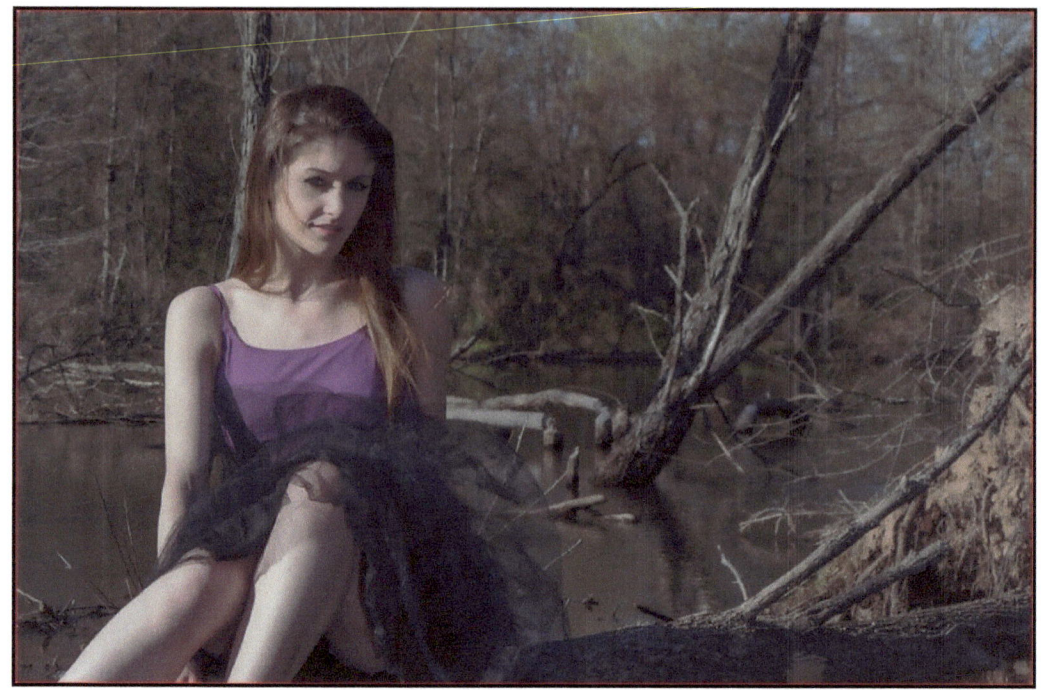

Fashion Portraits

Portrait lighting is ultrasoft and a keylight is placed right over the lens with a reflector just beneath the lens. Keylight is placed close to subject to get a softest effect. Makeup gives dimension and contouring to the subject face, with frontal lighting that relieves the roundness of the face roundness. Shaded cheekbones and both sides of the nose, give a better shape to the face.

For men's fashion portraits, ultra close up camera views, camera tilting, and very casual style of posing. Makeup is also applied for the desired effect.

SENIOR PORTRAITS

Teens and seniors are very conscious of how they look. It is important for a photographer to be well aware of the styles and latest fashions to help the seniors appear at their best, reassured and relaxed with perfect portraits. Seniors will want to be photographed in a number of outfits and variety of poses, and it is good to opt for a natural look. It might be a good idea to let the seniors bring in any props which will make them feel comfortable and add personality to the portrait.

This book will serve as a guide to all portrait photographers who want to refine their skills and learn the tricks of the trade for expert portrait photography.

ABOUT THE AUTHOR

Ryan Crane is a well-known name in international published photography. Ryan developed his photography skills through painstakingly long hours of research and trial and error. Having carved a niche in the world, he now aims to help others who are just starting to step into the world of photographic art. Visit ryancranephotography.com to start learning today! Click improveyourphotographyonline.com, if you are a photographer looking to improve their craft.

www.ingramcontent.com/pod-product-compliance
Lightning Source LLC
Chambersburg PA
CBHW040820200526
45159CB00024B/3057